One silent sleepless night
Spencer W. Kimball

Illustrations by Sherry Thompson

BOOKCRAFT, INC.
Salt Lake City, Utah

Library of Congress Catalog Card Number: 75-34832

ISBN 0-88494-291-0

Second Printing, 1975

LITHOGRAPHED IN U.S.A. BY
PUBLISHERS PRESS
SALT LAKE CITY, UTAH

This is a record of one silent, sleepless night which I spent in 1957 in a bedroom on the third floor of the Mission Home in New York City following major surgery in which I lost one vocal cord and part of another and then had staph infection following the surgery.

For all the long hours of the seemingly endless night I suffered and reminisced. When I arose I sat at my typewriter and wrote by the hour, at least partly to occupy the time and divert my attention from my pains and woes.

Sleepless! I hardly know why. There is pain, though it should have been deadened by the medication prescribed by the doctors. *Silent!* Because I can't make much sound. Oh, I can roll and tumble and walk the floor, but I can't even groan loudly enough to wake my companion. Nor would I wish to disturb her sleep, for she too has had a hectic two weeks and, like me, has lost much sleep. What a fix, when a man can't even groan aloud or grunt audibly— nor laugh, nor call, nor speak—just a tiny whisper!

It seems that the pain is less intense tonight; it is 8:30; I have had a heavy day; I am weary of body. Surely I will sleep all night.

Now I prepare to be gone all night. I lie on my back because this puts less pressure on the wound in my throat caused by the surgeon's taking one vocal cord and part of the other. I lie quietly. I will be sleeping soon, and before I know it the morning will be here and the exotic birds from Central Park across the way will be singing their crisp melodies.

Time passes. It seems a long time since I retired. My wife has set aside her book and turned out the light. As she did so she reached over and looked, and I was so still with my eyes closed that she supposed me to be asleep. I must not disturb her. She is tired tonight. I lie quiet, thinking. After a while her breath becomes heavier—she is asleep. Now I can turn over on my right side, and I'll be asleep in no time.

No time? But there is always time. Why, in the past month I've counted it, I've bathed in it, I've wasted it. Time? There has been an overabundance of it, but it seems to have merged with the eternities. Since that night in Memorial Hospital it has lost its bounds and limitations.

I saw it last, in normal form, in the operating room in Memorial Hospital in New York City under the glaring lights, among the glass cases of sharp, shining instruments, in the midst of white-clad and muzzled nurses and doctors with their needles and knives and bottles and bandages. There and then I lost contact with time.

What happened to it I do not know, unless it lost its life in that room of anaesthesia—unless perchance its body went down the drain with other priceless possessions and its spirit wafted on the wings of ether, departed for another world across the deserts where are found the "sands of time," over limitless vastnesses till it reached that

world of endlessness, hurled itself at the bastions of eternity, and embedded itself in the very foundations of immeasurableness.

"Time marches on," they say, but that night it ceased to march. Its feet had lost the rhythmic beat; it slowed its pace, stumbled, crawled a little on its leaden feet, and finally stopped.

It must be late by now. I'll get my wristwatch and see. (I must be very careful not to disturb Camilla. She needs her sleep.) It is only 9:02 P.M.! Well, the night is slowly wearing on.

I'll put the watch on. How glad I am that it has luminous hands and figures. That was a lucky day when the missionary took us to the watch-seller in Zurich. And when he brought out this particular watch I could see no other. Always I had bought for myself something inferior, but here— this watch was so elegant that all I needed was a little urging from my wife and I had made the purchase. How proud I have been of this possession!

But this watch, with radium-tipped hands, can be trouble too. There was the day when we were going through customs at New York two years ago. Camilla had passed through "a-sailing" with her armload, but when I went through the narrow passageway they stopped me and brought me back and tried a little gadget like a geiger counter on me to see what I had that set off some kind of vibration in their machine. I suppose it was the radium-tipped watch. Yes, most things can work for either good or evil. Water can flood a home or drown a child, or it can make the desert bloom as the rose on the mountain and give life to a thirsty soul. Fire can keep a person warm or burn him to death. Atomic power can destroy cities or

move ocean liners across the seas. And a watch can stop a man at customs or tell the time of night.

By the way, what *is* the time? I ask myself. I've been back to Switzerland, a very long way—surely it must be near midnight. Nine fifty-eight; or is it ten minutes to twelve? That surely is the hour hand nearing twelve! It is 9:58! Incredible!

I'll turn on my left side. I'll do it so carefully that Camilla will not hear nor feel the movement of the bed. The pillow is cool to my face. Surely now I'll sleep the rest of the night.....Why didn't the watchmaker put radium on the second hand? The other one just does not move. Why can't time pass quickly as it did in Arizona that night back in 1917?.....

The lovely lady who now sleeps in the other of the twin beds is with me back there. We are hanging on the long wooden gate across the driveway into her father's farm. The gate is old and weary. It hangs on the high post lazily, the post itself leaning a little as though bent with age. But it is something to lean against, and we have leaned on it many evenings. No wonder it is tired. Many sweet nothings have been said here, and tonight is special.

The eastern sky is brightening, and soon the moon peeps above the hills over Duncan way. Soon it is far enough in the sky to make the night nearly as bright as the day. At least it is bright for us. We walk slowly down the road a little distance to the railroad track where the road is raised as it crosses the tracks. We stand between the tracks in the moonlight; the romance which has been developing for some time reaches fruition; and we agree upon a definite engagement and arrange plans for an early marriage.

I stir. I am back in my bed here in New York City! I hope it's getting late. I look again at the Swiss watch. It is 10:04. Only six minutes have passed since I last looked! This is absurd. I must take the situation in hand. I'll use

all my power, breathe deeply, and just go to sleep. My back is cramped. I'll straighten out and sleep on my back.

If I could just sleep for an hour! If I just had someone to talk to! If I just had the light on so that my eyes could wander—but maybe I can see much more with my eyes closed! Yes, that is true. I can see that hospital room again and its cases of shiny instruments, and the bright lamps blinding me, and the nurses and doctors assembling about me. Apparently I am going to be the central figure in this "grand opening."

It would have been interesting to see them literally sew the soaker towels to my chin and neck so that they would not be moved out of place and in the way. It would have been still more interesting to see the balance of the cutting and sewing program. Why didn't they give me a local anaesthetic and a mirror and let me see what they were doing to me? Maybe I could have taken it. After all, I did stand by one day in Safford as an emergency assistant to the doctor when he amputated about 85 percent of a leg. It was done on the kitchen table with the extra boards in to make it long enough, and with only regular kitchen lights. I carried out the leg reverently when the saw and knife had done their work, and stood by to help in any way with the sewing and bandaging of the stub. Yes, I think I could take it.

My memory takes me back to the Safford hospital on another occasion when my cousin needed an emergency gall-bladder operation. Her husband was not there and her father would be too late coming from a distance. Since

climb down to repair the pump, or find the bucket when it falls off, or retrieve something which has fallen down the well. The water is cold enough to cover the alkaline taste. And the windmill—I must watch it and lock it tight when the wind blows hard or it will pump so hard and fast that it might break something. And even as a little boy I climb to the top many times in a gale to fix the wires, or put on the brakes. And the tank. Brother Woods helped Pa put it together, a wooden tank about six feet deep and ten feet in diameter. In summer when the air is dead the tank empties and then leaks until it soaks up again. When the wind blows much the tank fills and overflows, and the surplus runs around the house to water the numerous exotic trees and shrubs Pa has planted.

How grateful I am for this abundance of water. Now we just turn a tap, the trough fills, and the cows and horses have plenty. It seems they never drink nearly so much now as they used to when I had to pump every drop they drank. How thirsty they were then! How limitless were their bellies! And how hot the metal pump handle was in summer, and how cold on those early wintry mornings!

Now my mind runs to the outbuildings, and I see them all again clearly in the dark of my New York sickroom. There is the granary with its oft-replenished supply of corn and bran for the pigs and wheat for the chickens. On the shelf above are the fruit bottles full of wheat, half of them with lime in them and half without, as we experiment to see which way the wheat will remain weevil-free the longest.

There is the harness shed. Pa is very meticulous with the harnesses. They must always be hanging up when not on the horses. The collars must be smooth and clean, the bridles fitting just right, the blinds in place. The harness must be washed with Ivory soap frequently and then oiled, and I learn another important lesson: the leather equipment must never be dry and hard and curled.

There is the buggy shed. The surrey and the one-seated buggy must always be in shelter from storm and sun, and they must be clean. I learn to wash vehicles and grease them. In a little pocket on the right side of the building is the axle-grease can and dauber. I lift one side at a time to the wooden horse, remove the wheel, grease the axle carefully, replace the nut, and screw it on to keep it in place. The wagons must be similarly treated as often as needed. And they must be painted too. I learn while yet a very small boy how to buy and mix paint and apply it to body and wheels and framework. The hairline of trim paint must be applied with precision. The fences must all be whitewashed and the trellis painted green. The house, the big house, needs paint too, and I climb the high ladders and paint the gable ends of the house and the trim. Pa does most of it at first, then I gradually come into the program until it is my task almost exclusively. And the barn and granary and harness shed—all must be painted at intervals. Even the mangers.

Now I am back with the cows. Even at nine years I am milking all the cows. Sometimes there are two or three, sometimes as many as nine. My smaller sister Alice helps me milk—she is a good little worker. I don't mind the milking too much since I have found ways to break the monotony. Sometimes I squirt the stream of milk into the mouth of the cat. A few times I insert clean straws from the straw stack into the teats and let the milk run out without so much effort on my part. (I know I can't do this very often because it would spoil the teats.) Sometimes I learn the Ten Commandments and the Articles of Faith and other scriptures and repeat them over and over as I milk.

I recall that often I sang to the cows. I learned most of the songs usually sung in our meetings and this was a great blessing, for I have retained in my memory not only the scriptures but also those songs, so that even now at my age I can still sing most of the songs without a book—that is, I could before I came to this sickroom with my vocal cord removed.

Oh, I am back again! What a delightful visit I had in Thatcher! Maybe the night is nearly over. But no; the luminous hands say it is 10:45. It will be hours before dawn arrives. But maybe I can sleep now, after that happy visit in the land of memories.....

My wound is hurting again. It is nearly unbearable. I'll get up and put hot wet packs on the wound.....It takes a long time to get the hot water up the four stories, but here it is. There is some drainage and the warmth brings comfort, so I'll go back now and sleep the rest of the night. How blessed is sleep! I lie quietly on my back so that I will not pull and strain the stitches. My eyes are closed, the room is dark. This gives me unlimited vision and I seem unable to hold myself here.

I'm in Thatcher again in the old red schoolhouse. It is the morning recess, the fifteen-minute period for relaxation, but I'm a bit confused. I think it is noon, and I have so much to do to pump water for the stock and to feed the pigs as well as to eat my lunch that I must hurry. I run much of the way home and Ma sees me coming and meets me at the door. "What's the matter?" she asks anxiously. "Why are you running home at recess?" "Is it just recess?" I ask incredulously, and with a red face I rush back to the schoolground to find it deserted and into the schoolroom to find the children laughing at my error.

The night is wearing on. The New Yorkers about us on Park and Fifth Avenues in their tuxedos and evening dresses are still early in their evening's festivities.

I am wandering again, back to childhood. We are at a picnic, all the good Thatcher folks. We have come on horseback, in buggies and in wagons to old Cluff's ranch. We enjoy the great swings from the monumental cotton-woods. There is lemonade for sale. The picnic dinner is incomparable.

The swim in the pond is the ultimate—everybody goes in swimming. No skimpy bathing suits here—people are wearing dresses, stockings, and overalls. Father is such a good swimmer. How I wish I could swim as he does! All over the great pond he moves easily and seemingly without effort. Now he comes for me, his little boy. I am on his back with my arms around his neck so tightly that he must constantly warn me. The water is deep and I am scared,

and I plead with him to take me back to the shallow water. At last we feel ground, and I say, "I'm all right now, Pa," and I see him turn and swim off toward deep water. I start toward shore and step into a deep hole. Down, down, down! Water is filling my lungs.....I cannot scream! Why doesn't someone get help? Will they never rescue me? Someone has now seen my predicament. Pa has heard their screams and is after me. I am full of water and coughing, spitting, crying for a long time. I thought I was drowned.

But how did I get way down to Arizona again? O yes, I heard the whistle of a boat on the East River, which reminded me of the youngsters swimming in it and diving from the scraggy rocks. We saw them last week as we took the Circle trip around Manhattan Island. How I wish I could swim like those little urchins! If I could have swum like that when I was a child—and then my mind had relived the near-drowning experience in Arizona.

The pain is more than I can bear. The doctor gave me some Empirin pills, so I'll take one to relieve the pain, and then go to sleep.....After what seems like hours I am still turning and twisting. But at last the pain subsides; the pill has done its work. I sink into fitful sleep—I am so weary.

Finally I stir. I've been gone a long time. The birds soon will be announcing the coming of morning. I'll look at my faithful watch again. It is 11:15, or can't I read time any more? But at least I had a little sleep. Sleep? Well, it was a troubled sleep. I'm not sure I entirely let go. Why will my mind not sleep? Why must it wander?

A mosquito is buzzing near my ear. My neck will start its throbbing again if I slap at him. Let him suck—but then I hardly have blood to lose. Maybe I should have had that blood transfusion which the doctor offered me and which I refused, then I could spare a little for this beast. Mosquitos, fleas, bedbugs! Ugh!

How my mind flits about! What distances it does cover! Here I am at that little shack in the Ozarks where my missionary companion and I slept that night. The meeting in the schoolhouse in the clearing in the woods comes vividly to my mind—the dozens of curious friends, my timid request for a place to sleep, the invitation from this young man to go to their home, our gratitude. Again I retrace those steps.

We are closing the schoolhouse, walking through the forest with many people. Every once in a while a family goes off on a side trail and says, "Goodnight,you-all." Finally

all are gone but our own kind family. We are trying to follow the father with his lantern, all ten of us. Sometimes we step in the puddles, since we cannot see well. Miles, miles we travel. Could we still be in Missouri? Finally a dark square object looms up and announcement is made that this is the place.

It is a one-room frame dwelling. We look around quickly to see where ten people are going to sleep, for there is only one bed and one cot. (We don't mention that we have had nothing to eat all day, since we are so glad for a bed. They don't think of it, since they had their supper before going to the meeting.) It is late—bedtime. There is a hole in the corner of the rough ceiling, leading to the little attic under the sloping roof. The larger children, barefoot, climb up the corner without a ladder, putting their bare toes and fingers between the logs for holds, and up through the hole they go. The littlest ones are handed up and received into that dark space above. Finally the mother goes up the log corner and disappears.

We hear them jockeying for position above, hear them find their places. Then the father says to us, "That is your bed." What? Are we to take the only bed in the house? How kind can people be? The father and son are to sleep on the single cot while we stretch our tired limbs in the bed.

And now the battle of the night begins. The bedbugs come marching out for the night's forage. We think of the German Army. Could there be fewer bedbugs than an army of them? We fight and bleed. Surely all the bugs have deserted the family tonight and are seeking new blood, missionary blood!

Thatcher, oct. 30, 1

I love the name of Washington
I love my country too.
I love the Flag, The dear old Flag
Of red and white and blue,
          Spencer Kimball,
          age 8,
               Third grad,

I run quickly to the music and color and foreign atmosphere of Old Mexico, to the missionaries, the Saints, their sacrifices, their triumphs; I jump an ocean to the land of the Paradise of the Pacific. I am out waist-deep in the sea with numerous of my dark-skinned brethren. It is a hukelau. The nets have been cast far out in a big semicircle and we are pulling in the catch. Nearer and nearer come the fish. The waves throw us under, the weight of the pull trips us. We get wet, but it is such a novel and interesting experience! Finally we have pulled it in, and what an assortment of fish there is, big and little fish of every kind!

Then we are at the luau under the bowery made with tree limbs for shade. There is the barrel of poi, the uncooked fish, the salads and the fruits. What a meal! There is the pageant and dance arranged for us by this happy laughing people. We are in the meetings and hear their testimonies

34

and we preach to them and encourage them......(But the doctors make no promises that I shall ever be able to do so again.)

I flit here and there, across two oceans and a continent, and am in Finland with a youth conference of these strong sweet youth of little Finland; I am preaching at Narvik in the far north, where there is no darkness; I am dedicating chapels in Sweden; I am moving rapidly in the tiny local car through England, Scotland and Wales, teaching, preaching, exhorting. I am in Ireland trying with my small voice to compete with the Orangemen's parade in the street below. I am instructing a group of missionaries in Holland. I am holding conference in Berlin with the local full-time missionaries who have come from behind the Iron Curtain to be instructed and to bear their testimonies.

I am in Paris at a conference of French, Belgian and Swiss youth; in faraway Vienna, where the Russian occupation forces are still in evidence; and finally in Switzerland with the thousand missionaries and thousands of Saints at the new temple, and with the prophet and some of my brethren at the dedication service, and I speak to the many who are present.

Shall I ever speak at another temple dedication? Shall I ever preach again? I force myself back from pleasant memories to a future which looks nearly as dark as this room. It must be nearly morning. I must have spent much

time in those distant wanderings. I must have slept a little too, for New York life outside the window is quieting a little. There are fewer taxis swishing by, less laughter floating on the night air, not so many trucks and buses passing. Yes, it is 1:30. I am grateful that some time has passed.

I walk the floor. (It is covered with a deep rug, so my movements are noiseless.) This helps a little. I lean over the metal balustrade and watch the traffic below, which is thinning perceptibly. I wet-pack my wound. I take a warm bath and, lo and behold, I go to sleep!.....

Nearly an hour has passed. It is 2:25. Maybe another wet-pack operation will achieve the same results and take an hour from the timeless night.....But sleep has fled. Time is slow, slow as the hands on the tower clock over there in the New York skyline to the southwest of the Memorial Hospital. My mind wanders again.

I sit out again in memory those nights following the operation when I couldn't sleep—out on the west porch of

the hospital. The skyline is beautiful. There is the Empire State Building with hundreds of lights all night—yes, all night, for I see them every hour, from dusk to dawn; and the Chrysler Building; and the others, one after another; and down low under one of the tallest buildings a little one, probably not over thirty-five or forty stories high. In the hazy night it looks like I.B.M. on one level and on the other a changing figure. What is it? Oh, yes, it is a time-ticker.

I sit out on the porch, the west porch at Memorial Hospital, my head in my hands. A faint breeze stirs. I walk the hall on floor nine and return to sit out on the porch again and watch the changing figures of time. My eyes become accustomed to them and to the haze. It is 2:46. After a time it goes off and flashes back on again. It is 2:47. I count sixty, but it doesn't change. I counted too fast. I'll try again very slowly. It shifts again; it is now 2:48. I'll count minutes instead of counting sheep. But such a long time elapses before it is 2:49 and 2:50; then I walk slowly up the hall and back, and it is still only 2:59. I'll wait at least till 3:00 before I return to bed. I am unable to find any more sixty-second minutes or sixty-minute hours or twenty-four-hour days. All are endless. What has happened to normal time?

But that was at the hospital. That is across town. I'm back in the bed at 973 Fifth Avenue.

My mind flits from one thing to another and settles on childhood experiences again. I am back in Thatcher in the early days when we pumped water for the stock and for the plants. The Union Irrigation Canal is only a block from us. It is summer and very dry. The clouds have missed us for months, the river is sandy, the upper canals run no water; only the Union has a little trickle in it.

I drive the cows and lead the horses to drink from the pools. I drive the horse to pull the lizard, the forked log on which we move the barrel of water. The lizard is dragged on the ground. I drive it down into the canal and fill the barrel with the bucket, put a canvas over the barrel and then a metal hoop over that to keep the precious water from sloshing out. I drive the lizard around the yard and apportion the precious liquid out to the trees and plants, being careful to make trenches around the roots of each so that there will be no loss of this life-giving element. And precious fruit trees and ornamental trees and shrubs are kept alive in this way till it rains and canal water is again available.

We have some wonderful fruit trees which give a bounteous crop to be bottled and stored for winter use for a large family of ever-hungry children. I can almost taste those delicious peaches now, peaches of many varieties, some of which we sell, using the proceeds to buy school books and clothing; the Bartlett pears, the early plums, the pie cherries which come early, and even the sour Pottowatomie plums, which are among the first to come when we children are so hungry for fruit that we will eat almost anything. There are the crab apples which also come early, and the currants. How could one ever satisfy his appetite with the small currants, especially when they are constantly

picked over by many hungry little folks and eaten as fast as they are turning ripe? There are some blackberries growing wild along the ditch bank, though they are few and far between. But in the late summer there is an abundance of peaches, apples, pears. I remember too the quince, which is so dry and puckery but which makes such tasty preserves. All this delicious fruit comes at a cost.

Sometimes I wish that the trees were not so prolific, for it falls to my lot to pick up the decaying windfalls for the numerous pigs we always have. The spoiling fruit I pick up in the honey cans which, when emptied, I use to carry slop and other feed to the pigs. For a handle, I either fasten wire across the can or nail a round piece of wood across.

I learn as a small boy to trim the trees and to ride the horse while Pa or my older brothers plow the furrows for watering the trees. It is my job to cut the weeds—endless weeds. Why cut them? for they will only grow again. Sunflowers, cockleburrs, red roots—or "pig weeds," as we call them. I carry the "pig weeds" to the hogs and some also to the cows, as they eat them with relish if the weeds are young and fresh. Then, when the fruit season is well advanced and the ground is covered with decaying fruit, we turn the hogs into the orchard.

Now I have the job once more of helping to fence the orchard with pig wire and then helping to maintain the fence. The pigs are always getting out and bothering the neighbors. Why won't they stay in this fruitful field? There are lots of weeds, fruit, and grass here, even more than in the neighbors' smaller yards, but somehow they seem to always want to go visiting. There are always holes to plug in the fence, for the forty or fifty hogs seem always to be finding a hole or making one.

I learn also how to butcher hogs, for we produce our own meat. I watch Pa and the older boys so many times that I can finally do it myself with some help. I know just where to hit the hog with the heavy sledgehammer. One stroke fells it and it is dead. We drag it to the tree, cut the hocks, spread its hind feet apart with a stick sharpened on each end, pull the hog up the limb till its head is off the ground, remove the entrails, wash it clean. The metal tub is full of scalding water into which the body is dipped; then with butcher knives we work rapidly to scrape all the hair off. We then hang the pig in the tree above to cool.

The head-cheese and the sausages made from this animal will be beyond compare. But at the time, one less pig to feed is the thought that enters my mind—one less squealing pig. Pa says that the pigs must be hungry when they squeal, but I learn that they squeal the minute they see me at any distance.

The scene closes and some sharp pains bring me back to my bed in the Fifth Avenue room we occupy. Time?

47

Yes, I'll look again. It is five minutes to four. I turn over to the right, then to the left, and upon my back, over and over. There seems to be no comfortable place. I'll take another warm bath and go to sleep for the rest of the night.

The drawing of the warm water up four stories, a slow deliberate soaking, a long, extra-good drying, and wet-packing the wound—these all take some time but bring no sleep. I lie down again at 4:20. I try to sleep but I find myself wondering what I shall do when I return to Salt Lake City. Shall I ever fit into the program again, the great work to which I was called by the Lord through President Heber J. Grant back in 1943? And with this thought I'm back in Arizona again.

The phone is ringing, and now President J. Reuben Clark, Jr., first counselor in the First Presidency, is informing me that I have been called to fill the position in the Quorum of the Twelve Apostles left vacant by Elder Sylvester Q. Cannon when he died recently. I cannot believe my ears. My family members are aghast and have the same difficulty in believing. Surely I could not have heard correctly.

I lie in bed and reminisce and go through those difficult days of sleeplessness and shock and wonderment, and the visit to Salt Lake City and to the office of President David O. McKay, the other counselor to President Grant. He assures me that I am rightly called of God to this great work. I visit with President Grant, who is ill. He tells me of my father and their boyhood associations, he kisses me on the forehead and assures me that I have received a divine call. I see with unbelieving eyes the big headlines in the newspaper.

I seem dazed again as once more I travel this road. I follow the months—the moving to headquarters; the difficulty in getting living accommodation; the first assignments, then the constant assignments every week preaching to thousands; the interviewing of prospective missionaries; the organizing of stakes and missions; the receptive people, the kind, thoughtful people; the glorious work which comes to mean so much to me, even more than life itself. And I wonder on my bed in these still small hours, Shall I ever return to such activity with the loss of my vocal cord and my weak, poor voice? Will the Brethren give me service? Will my gruff fringe voice be an affront to the people? Will I repel people like a stammerer?

With these thoughts sleep moves further and further away, for these are emotional blocks. The time? Oh, yes. The time is 4:40. Since I can't sleep I might just as well dream—daydream if not night dream.

51

I return to my childhood and my first long trip. My father is a most gracious host. He takes me with him to Salt Lake City to General Conference. I am ten. We go via Bowie, Los Angeles, and San Francisco, since there is no "Short Line" from Los Angeles to Salt Lake City. We visit the mission home of the California Mission at San Francisco. He takes me to Cliff Point and lets me ride many of the concessions, which I shall never forget. I see the seals and many things to tell my less fortunate brothers and sisters. (My mother had 11 children.) This is in 1906. It would only be weeks until San Francisco would be in flames and ashes and debris. I would never see that San Francisco again.

In Salt Lake City we stay with Aunt Alice, Pa's twin sister. She is the wife of Joseph F. Smith, President of the Church, and I see his love and appreciation for his family as he comes into the home and kisses each one there. What a beautiful relationship between parents and children! And what a great man! And the box at the old Salt Lake Theatre is available to Aunt Alice, and I get to sit in the theatre with the prophet of the Lord. I do not remember anything about the play, but I remember the President coming in after the family has arrived; and he kisses them all round and enjoys being with them.

We go back across Nevada, a long, long ride. We stop in San Francisco and again in Los Angeles. We are nearing home after an absence of a month. I can hardly wait. The forty miles on the last lap from Bowie seems interminable. At last comes the Gila Valley in its greenness, and Thatcher, and the family!

The watch moves slowly on. It is five o'clock. Am I mistaken about what seems to be a lessening of the darkness? It won't be long now. Time to dream some more. Amazing how fast one can move about in thought, eliminating space and time.

I skip distance and time and am in Salt Lake again. The year is 1924. I have leave of absence from the Safford, Arizona, bank where I am employed. I am nurse to my dying father on 817 First Avenue. We have his funeral in the 27th Ward with Church leaders present. We take the body home to Thatcher, accompanied by President Heber J. Grant, who speaks at the funeral there and attends the burial.

A couple of hours after the burial we are in a stake conference especially called. Brother Harry L. Payne is presented to the people as the new president of the stake to succeed Father, and I am sustained as second counselor to him. I am dazed. My mind is in a whirl. So much has happened so rapidly these past few days. Am I dreaming? My brothers think it too great a responsibility for a boy of twenty-nine. "It will make him old before his time," they say, and the noble President of the Church replies, "Spencer doesn't need to accept the call if he doesn't want it," and that ends the matter, for the boys know that I will accept every Church responsibility given me.

All the family is together again for the first time in many years—that is, all the living ones: Clare, Gordon, Dell, Alice, Helen and myself, five girls having died prior to this date. Our father is buried. His second wife has been buried for a couple of years. His third wife, Aunt Mary, who has been married to him only a year, is with us but she will return to Salt Lake City to live. We will go our several ways tomorrow.

The house is to be sold and all the contents distributed and disposed of. We appraise the personal things and divide them. Never were brothers and sisters less selfish. Instead of saying, "I want this," each one is trying to pass to the others the most valuable things, the ones with the most sentiment attached. The rugs, the books, the ornaments, the clocks, the numerous things of sentimental and monetary value are distributed till all six receive a full and equal share and no one is discriminated against. What a world this would be if all brothers and sisters were so unselfish! I have seen quite the opposite in many families when such a situation arose.

I go back again in time, nineteen years further back in a fleeting second, and feel the strange dead feeling one morning when I come to breakfast with my face feeling tight. The other youngsters are laughing at me. ''Look at Spencer's face,'' and such a sight it is! One side is paralyzed. I cannot laugh or move my lips. I talk with some difficulty. My eye has no expression. I cannot whistle. There is consternation in all the group when the seriousness of it is realized. We consult our family general practitioner. He prescribes some liniment which I rub on my face. I am administered to and fervent prayers are offered on my behalf. The blessing comes gradually. In months the deadness has disappeared and normal life is restored to the face; and after another half-century has passed into history there will be no return of the malady.

Time to dream some more? Yes. No perceptible light yet here on Fifth Avenue. I'll go back to Arizona.

I am on the basketball court. We play in our overalls and shirts with cheap rubber shoes and with basketballs of our own buying. We have beaten Globe High School on our dirt court, and we have defeated Safford and other high schools. Now, tonight, we Academy boys are playing the University of Arizona team.

It is a great occasion. Many people come tonight who have never been before. Some of the townsmen say basketball is a girl's game, but nevertheless they come in large numbers tonight. Our court is not quite regulation. We are used to it, our opponents are not. I have special luck with my shots tonight, the ball goes through the hoop again and again, and the game ends with our high school team the victors against the college team. I am the smallest player and the youngest on the team. I have piled up the most points through the efforts of the whole team in protecting me and feeding the ball to me. I am on the shoulders of the big fellows of the Academy. They are parading me around the hall to my consternation and embarrassment.

I like basketball. I would rather play this game than eat, and I am a growing boy with a growing appetite. But basketball gives me some of my most trying situations. We have to do all our practicing after school, and milking

time comes all too soon every day. I play till the last possible minute, then take just a few more throws; and when I get home, after running most of the way, I find the milk customers sitting on the bench at the back door waiting, waiting for their milk. We sell milk to neighbors, and they come for it. The delay for customers who are standing around and waiting around night after night must be far more exasperating than I can ever realize. Because I score time and time again it always seems that I can play just another minute without overrunning time, and my "milking" memory is short when I am enjoying myself so much on the basketball court.

We go to Clifton to meet the high school team there. That high school, supported in large part by the mines in those camps, has a smooth floor to play on, and the boys have suits given them and their shoes have thick rubber soles which give traction. Our shoes are worn smooth, and while we slide and slip around the floor our opponents run up a score on us. Wait till we get them on our dirt court at the Academy!

I am back to the present again in New York City. The faintest first indications of the morn seem to be there. Am I mistaken? No, the greying night is accompanied by sweet music, the songs of birds. Exotic birds from Central Park across the street are near, perhaps on the ledge of the nearby house. Their chirps and whistles are music to my ears. They divert my thoughts back to the present, and they mean that the day breaks. Trucks are passing more often now and the buses are increasing their schedule. A few jolly parties are returning to their apartments to go to bed after their night's revelry.

The room lightens. I can see the walls, the furniture, the decorations. I am back in the apartment, I can hold my thoughts from winging. Others are stirring in the house. The night is gone. The day is here. Life is better. What a difference between night and day! Pain is reduced. I can now make plans for the day before me, and "One Silent Night" becomes history.

Some days have passed. Last night I had a full night of sleep without medication. How glorious! The pigeons are cooing more pleasantly this morning. The Central Park birds are singing more lustily. Pain, the ugly, sadistic companion of the past three weeks, has moved out to give place first to the mild-mannered gentleman Distress, which in turn has now given way to the friendly person Comfort. And with comfort comes peace, and with peace a return of memory of a certain Time, the Time with which I was formerly acquainted; the Time which has now rubbed its eyes, taken a deep breath, saluted, clicked its heels, and comes marching its way back into the normal sixty-second minutes and sixty-minute hours and twenty-four-hour days.

TIME has been resurrected, peace restored, and life is good again!

Or